# Save
# The Earth

## by Jeri Lee C.Ht.

ISBN: 9798355344870

With respect for our planet and the disrespect of how its population has treated it either knowingly or unconsciously, I believe we all share the guilt of its destruction and the responsibility of its rescue. I share with you the echoing voices of two of its most recent authorities on the subject and pledge to do my part in helping the planet help itself.

Albert Einstein said: The world will not be destroyed by those who do evil, but by those who watch them without doing anything. Everything that exists in your life, does so because of two things: something you did or something you didn't do. Failure is success in progress.

Stephen Hawking said: Remember to look up at the stars and not down at your feet. Try to make sense of what you see and hold on to that childlike wonder about what makes the universe exist. It is very important for young people to keep their sense of wonder and keep asking why.

We are only the temporary custodians of the particles of which we are made. They will go on to lead a future existence in the enormous universe that made them.

With this series of books Save the Planet, I hope you share these values with me. I was born in 1939 and have watched the planet get small enough to fit into your living room while losing the true meaning of nature. So I am requesting your help in rectifying the damage.

Sample Page

Sample Page

SAVE THE
PLANET

LET THERE BE PEACE
ON EARTH
AND
LET IT BEGIN
WITH ME

OUR FUTURE

IS IN

OUR HANDS

SAVE THE EARTH

Save our Planet

SAVE THE BEES

SAVE OUR
PLANET

OCT
4TH
World
Animal Day
Save The
Amazon

SAVE
OCEAN

SWEET ANGEL
MEOW
PRINCESS DRAGON

SAVE
THE
SEA

WORLD
TURTLE DAY

SAVE THE EARTH

OUR FUTURE
IS IN
OUR HANDS

LET THERE
BE PEACE
ON EARTH
AND
LET IT BEGIN
WITH ME

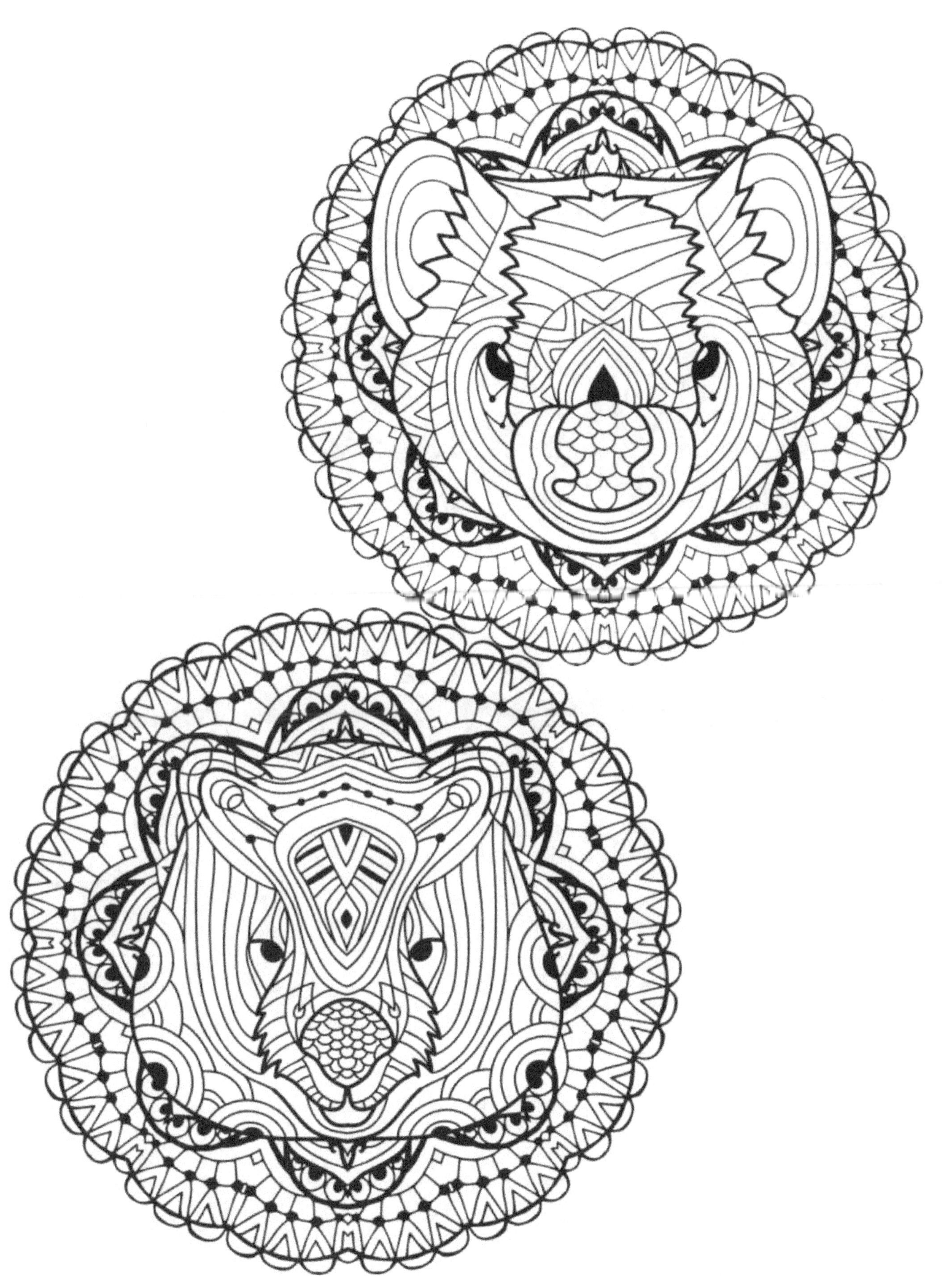

World
Wildlife
Day

save the Bees

SAVE the PLANET

SAVE
KOALA

SAVE THE
KOALA
DAY
SEPTEMBER 24

SAVE THE WILDLIFE
OF AFRICA

KEEP the OCEAN

CLEAN

LET THERE BE PEACE ON EARTH
AND LET IT BEGIN WITH ME

save the planet

SAVE THE PLANET
SAVE OURSELVES

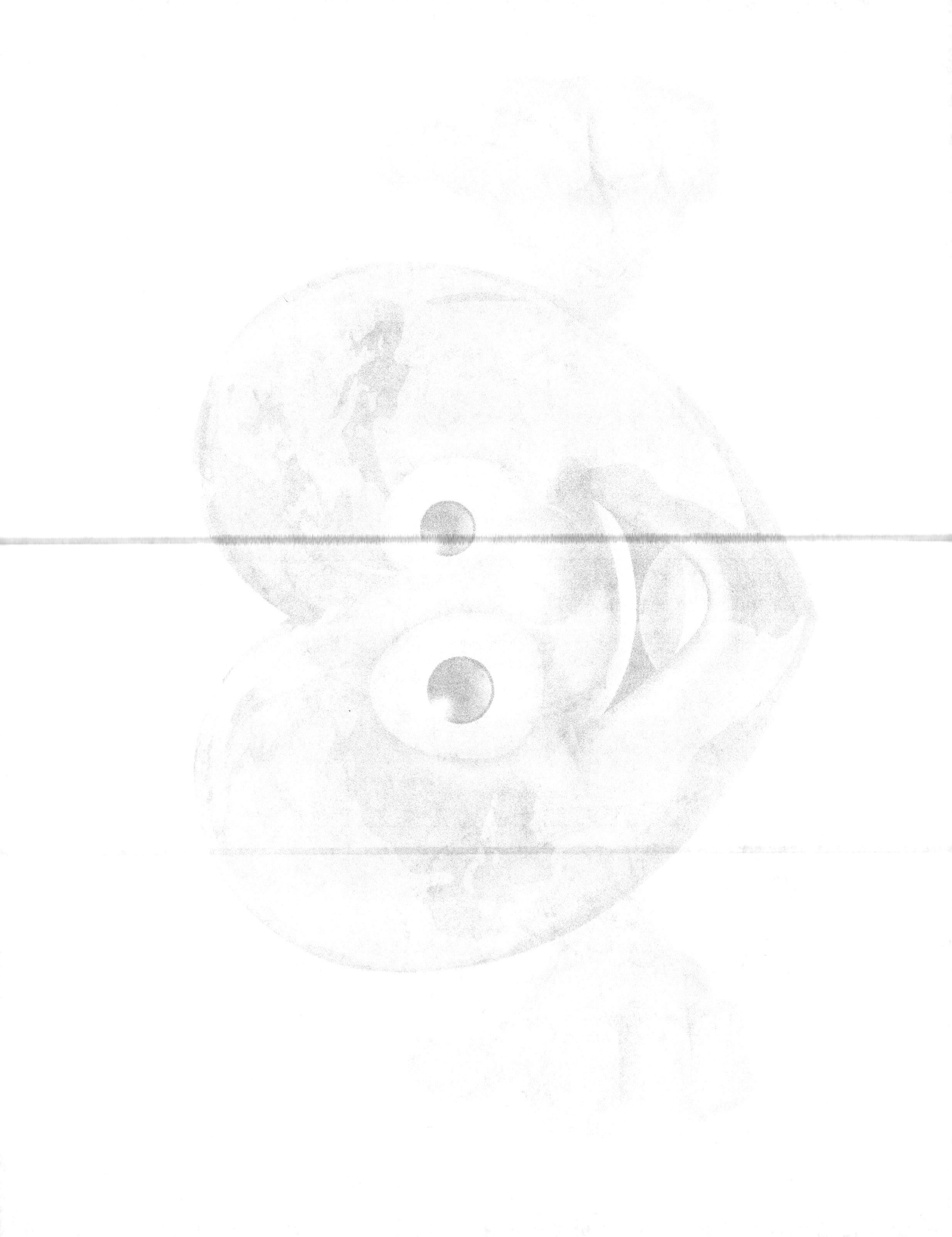

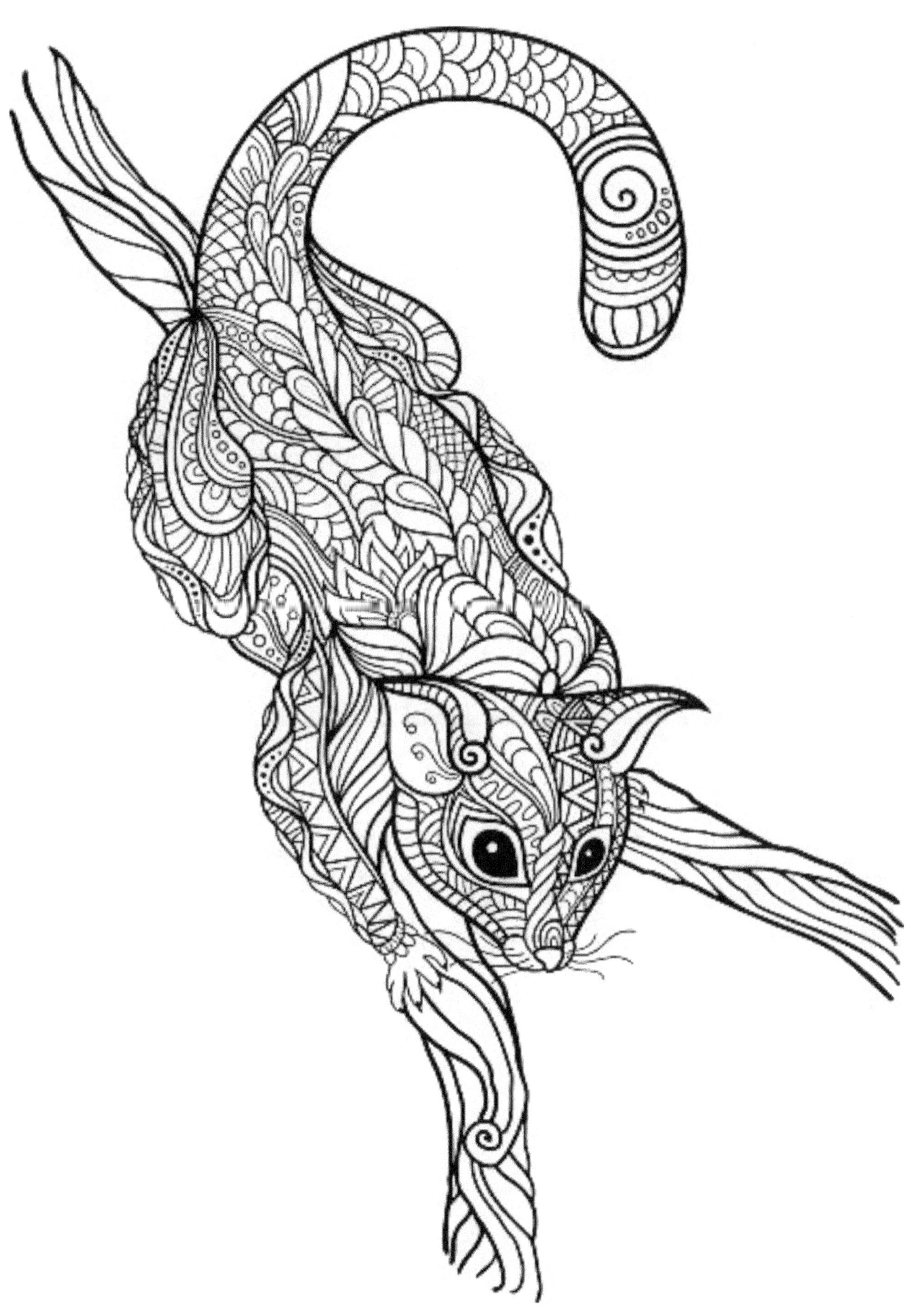

JUST
HONEY
SINCE
30mln. YEARS
A.D.

Too
hot

WORLD TURTLE DAY 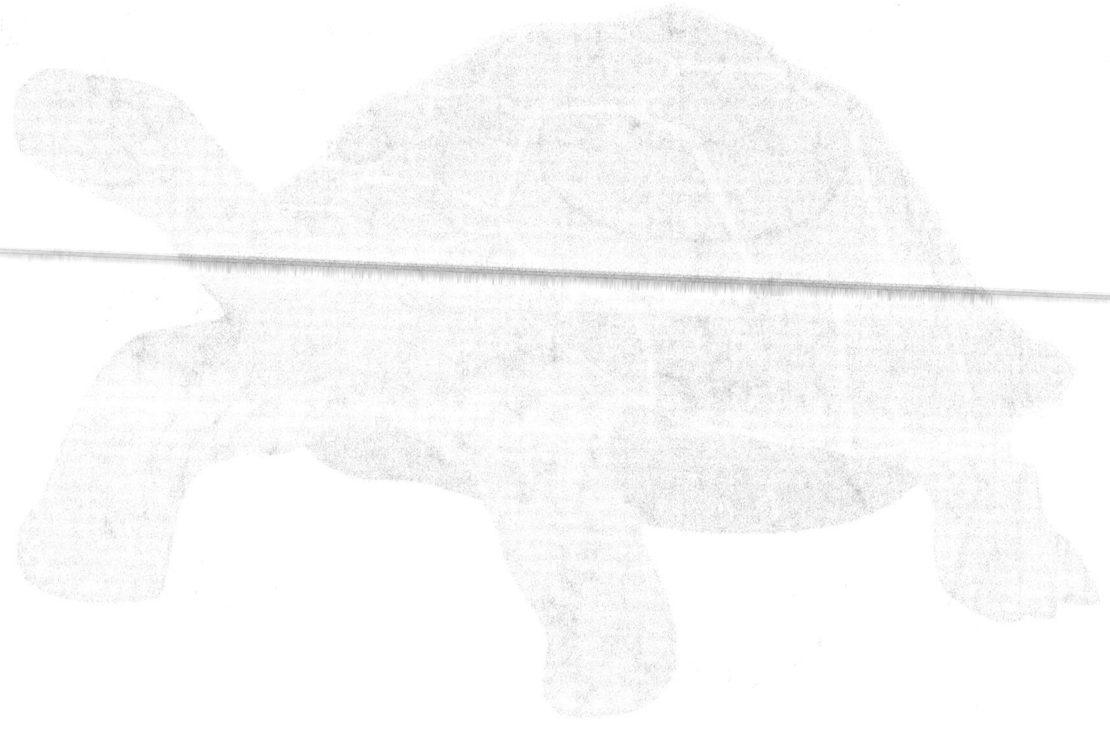
MAY 23

SAVE
OUR PLANET

African Elephant

Asian Elephant

# You Might Enjoy

## Other Coloring Books

Save the Planet Series
Family Pets Series
Match the Colors Series
Fantasy Series
Flowers & Birds Series
Adult Coloring Book Series

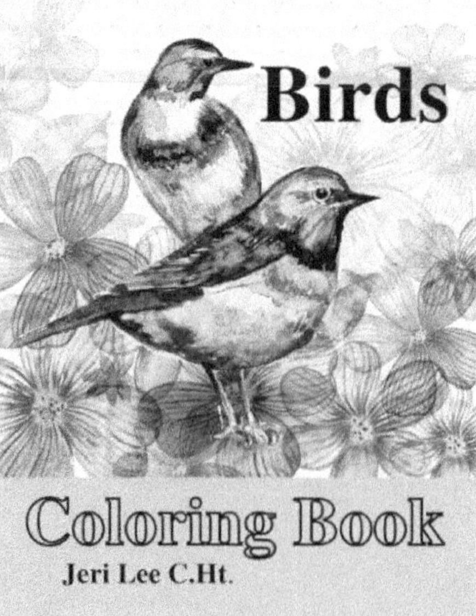

# **Author**
## and
## **Artist**
## Jeri LeeC.Ht.

Early education is fundamental for the children in our life. The ABCs and 1-2-3s we teach them are the building blocks of their future. We first give them love and care. Then we teach them to walk and talk and right from wrong. Next is their formal education and how to socialize in their environment. It is here that my books can assist. As a mother, grandmother, and great-grandmother, I know that all kids relate to animals, and the first ones they meet are their household pets. Then as they venture out, they meet Farm animals and learn new words like duck, pig, horses, and cows, and they soon discover the habits, sounds, and colors of their new friends. Then a visit to the Zoo introduces them to the world of Nature, and it is essential to teach them to respect without touching our natural environment.

I grew up on a farm and have lived on one most of my life, so it's a subject that comes easy. My coloring books are designed to teach kids to respect the world they live in.

They are published in collectible series with different coloring pages for different ages and interests.

If you like this book, please follow my other series, and if you would give me a good review as an author, I would greatly appreciate it.

# UNIVERSAL

# PEACE

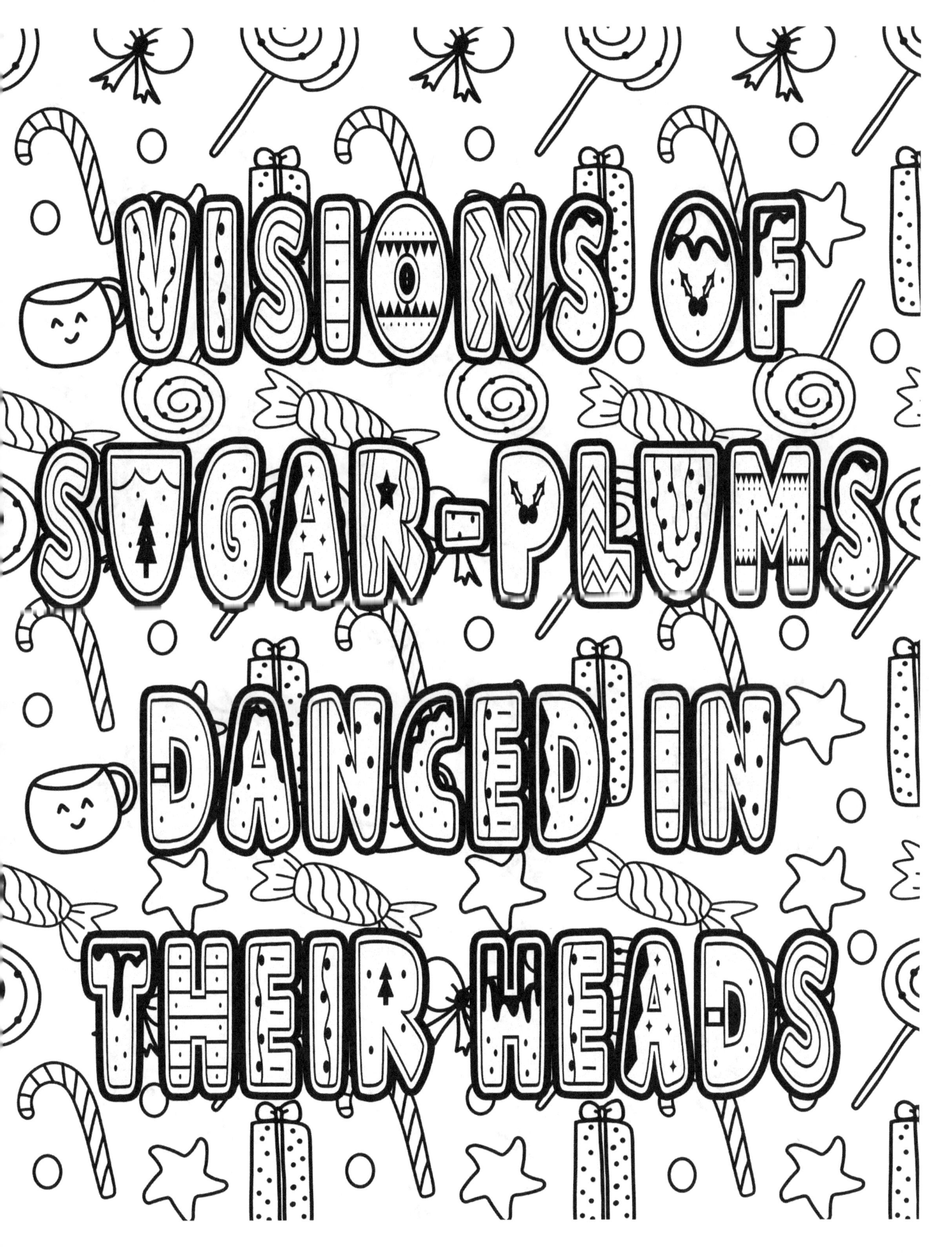

VISIONS OF
SUGAR-PLUMS
DANCED IN
THEIR HEADS

MERRY
TRIBE

LET
IT
SNOW

Dear Santa,
define
"Naughty"

Christmas
Vibes

Dreaming
of a white
Christmas

IT'S THE MOST WONDERFUL TIME OF THE YEAR

JINGLE
BELLS

SILENT
NIGHT

SANTA CLAUS
IS COMING
TO TOWN

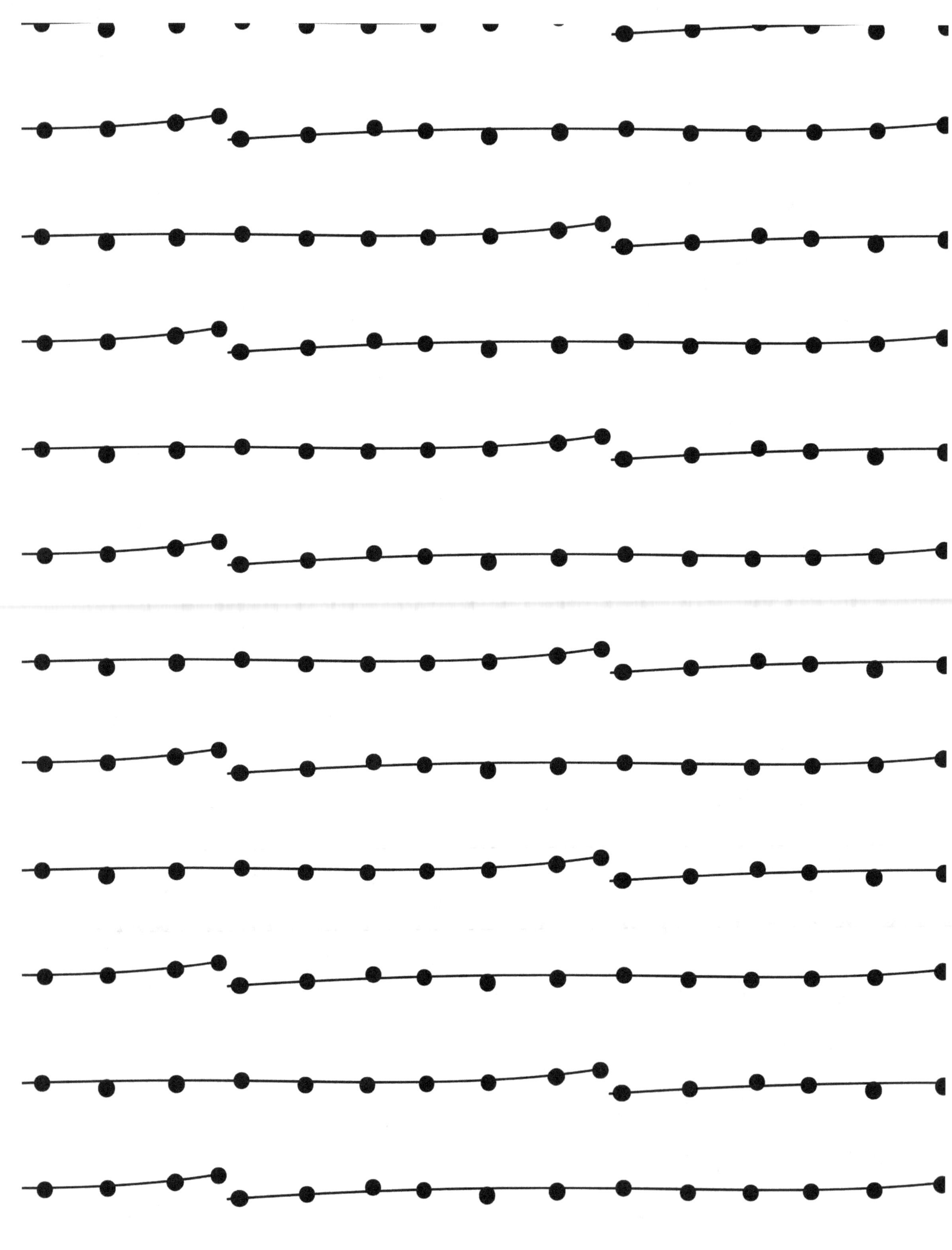

BAH
HUMBUG

HO HO HO
HO HO HO
HO HO HO
HO HO HO
HO HO HO
HO HO HO
HO HO HO
HO HO HO

DECK
THE
HALLS

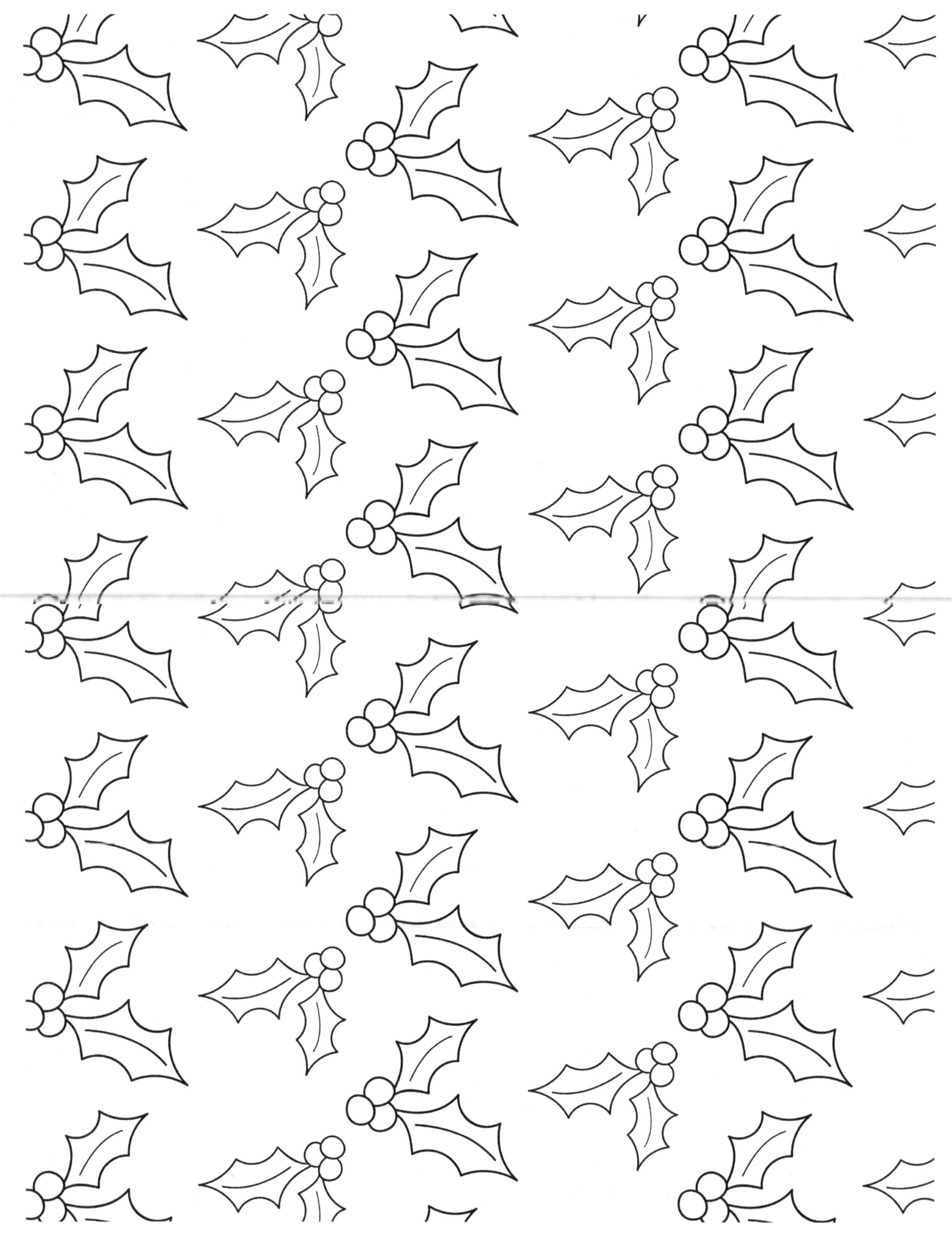

HERE
COMES
SANTA
CLAUS

MERRY
CHRISTMAS
YA FILTHY
ANIMAL

JOY
TO THE
WORLD

HOLLY
JOLLY

HAPPY
HOLIDAYS

Jingle
all the
way